Nita Me

Great Ideas

Beauty Cooking & Household Tips

Nita Mehta

B.Sc. (Home Science), M.Sc. (Food and Nutrition), Gold Medalist

SNAB
Publishers Pvt Ltd

Nita Mehta's **Great Ideas** Beauty Cooking & Household Tips

© Copyright 2000-2009 **SNAB** Publishers Pvt Ltd

5th Print 2009

ISBN 978-81-86004-84-5

Food Styling and Photography: **SNAB** Excellence in Books

Layout and Laser Typesetting :

National Information Technology Academy
3A/3, Asaf Ali Road
New Delhi-110002
N.I.T.A.
☎ 23252948

Published by :

SNAB
Excellence in Books
Publishers Pvt. Ltd.
3A/3 Asaf Ali Road,
New Delhi - 110002
Tel: 23252948, 23250091
Telefax:91-11-23250091

Contributing Writers :
Anurag Mehta
Subhash Mehta

Editorial & Proofreading :
Rakesh
Ramesh

Editorial and Marketing office:
E-159, Greater Kailash-II, N.Delhi-48
Fax: 91-11-29225218, 29229558
Tel: 91-11-29214011, 29218574
E-Mail: nitamehta@email.com
nitamehta@nitamehta.com
Website: http://www.nitamehta.com
Website: http://www.snabindia.com

Distributed by :

THE VARIETY BOOK DEPOT
A.V.G. Bhavan, M 3 Con Circus,
New Delhi - 110 001
Tel : 23417175, 23412567; Fax : 23415335
Email: varietybookdepot@rediffmail.com

Printed by :

DEVTECH PUBLISHERS & PRINTERS PVT LTD

Rs. 89/-

Contents

Foreword

Great ideas will transform any woman into a special woman. Become simply beautiful by discovering the natural beauty secrets — Beauty Ideas. Win your man's heart through his stomach by learning all the tricks to cook a delicious meal — Cooking Tips. Lastly, give your family a caring home which is inviting, warm and comfortable, making it truly, home sweet home — Home-Keeping Pointers. Be a complete woman, a woman of substance!

All the ingredients required for the ideas/tips presented herein are available generally on your kitchen shelf or easily and readily available from general stores. These were always available but you never knew how to use them. This book guides you to make the best use of these.

Nita Mehta

Handy Hints

- To prepare your natural beauty packs, if you need **juice** of anything, **finely grate** the fruit or vegetable — like cucumber (kheera), radish (mooli), potato, tomato etc. and then **squeeze** it within your palm (mutthi) to get juice.

- The juice should be taken out fresh and used immediately otherwise it loses most of it's value on keeping. Most of the vitamin C gets destroyed by atmospheric oxidation on keeping.

- To get pulp of a fruit, say for papaya or banana, grate a piece finely and then mash with a spoon.

- Whatever treatment you decide, stick to it and follow it regularly for a month to get lasting effects.

HAIR

Treat your hair gently and with care. Never comb very wet hair. Combing and brushing should be done when the scalp is at least partially dry. Use a wide toothed comb on your hair first, when the hair is still wet. Drying the hair calls for care. Avoid electric driers. Just wrap your hair with a dry towel and let it absorb the water. Don't scrub-dry as that would put tension at the hair roots, pulling out some hair and weakening others. Remember, the scalp's hold on hair is weaker when it is wet.

Natural Hair Colouring

♦ **Roast 2-3 tbsp of amla powder** till black and add to henna (mehandi). Soak overnight. You will get a copperish colour on your hair due to the **roasted amla powder**.

♦ For a rich copper colour, add a **1 tsp of eucalyptus (nilgiri) oil** to henna (mehandi) before applying.

♦ Boil the **outer cover of a dark onion** in a cup of water for a few minutes till it becomes half in quantity. Remove from fire and add **2 tsp of glycerine**. Cool. Divide hair into sections and apply with cotton wool. Massage well. Wash your hair when dry to get a reddish tint on your hair.

Prevent Greying of Hair

To prevent early greying of hair, take **1 cup of strong black tea** (without milk), and to this add **1 tbsp of salt.** When cold, strain the tea and apply it on the roots with cotton wool. Leave it on for an hour, then wash it off. **Do not shampoo it.** I frequently use the left over tea in the teapot for my hair.

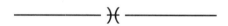

The cure or at least the slowing down of grey hair and falling off of hair can be effected by the use of **amla.** Regular massage of **amla ground to paste** and rubbed into the scalp has worked wonders in many cases, frequently reversing the process of greying or falling off of hair.

Removing Dandruff

Keep the **rice water (kanji)** after straining the cooked rice. If **kept overnight** and applied on the scalp next day, it will remove dandruff from the hair.

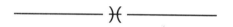

To treat dandruff, mix **1 tbsp of lemon juice and 2 tbsp of coconut oil** and massage it into the scalp. Leave it on for about 2 hours, then wash your hair with warm water. Dry it well with a soft towel before brushing the hair.

Hair Falling and Thinning

◆ Mix **juice of 1 lemon** with **2 tbsp of thick coconut milk.** Rub well into scalp. Leave for one hour. Repeat once a week.

◆ Soak **methi dana (fenugreek seeds)** in water for 2-3 hours and grind to a fine, thin **paste.** Divide hair into sections and apply with a hair brush. Wash after 1-2 hours.

◆ For falling hair and dandruff, beat **2 eggs** and add **2 tbsp of water** to it. Rinse hair to make it wet. Divide hair into sections and apply with a hair brush. Massage your scalp and leave it on for 20 minutes. Rinse the hair with luke warm water.

Thick, Lustrous Hair

If you want your hair to be long and lustrous, boil **2-3 handfuls of celery leaves** in water, remove from fire and cool. Strain out the water and add **juice of 1 lemon** to it. Rinse hair with this mixture after washing your hair.

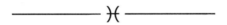

To develop long and lustrous hair, wash the head frequently with a mixture of **3-4 tbsp besan (Bengal gram flour) mixed with 1 cup curd.**

Face and Skin

♦ Never forget the neck in all the face treatments, as it shows the same telltale signs as the face.

♦ Apply the pastes and juices on an absolutely clean skin with a face brush.

♦ Do not talk when you have applied some thing on your face.

♦ For normal or dry skins, use milk or curd to make your pastes. Avoid lemon juice as it tends to dry the skin further. For oily skins, lemon juice is good.

Clear Pimples

- Wash and grind a few fresh **poodina (mint)** leaves to a smooth paste. Apply and leave for ½ hour or apply every night before going to sleep. This helps in getting rid of pimples along with the blemishes.

- Rub scrapped **karela (bitter gourd)** peels over the face to keep black heads and pimples away.

- To remove marks left by pimples, mix **1 tsp mooli (radish)** juice with **1 tsp lassi (buttermilk).** Apply to the face with a face brush and wash off after 1 hour.

Clear Blemishes and Scars from Face

Clean face with cotton wool dipped in **rose water** 1-2 times a day. It clears up and brightens the face.

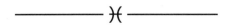

Blanch (soak and peel) a few **almonds.** Grind to a fine **paste** with **2 tbsp milk** and **1 tbsp** each of **orange juice and carrot juice.** Apply with a face brush on the face and neck. Leave for ½ hour, then wash off.

Take the pulp of a **ripe tomato.** Add a **few drops of lemon juice.** Rub on the face and neck. Leave for 20-25 minutes. Wash off.

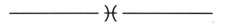

If your skin is **dry,** rub a stick of **sandalwood** in **milk** and if your skin is **oily,** rub it in **rose water** and then apply on face. Leave for 1 hour and then wash with cold water.

Smooth and Soft Skin

- Grind **1 tsp chironji** to a paste. Mix **1 tsp** each of **milk** and **curd.** Apply and leave for 20 minutes before washing off.

- To **1 tsp** of **carrot juice**, (grate some carrot and squeeze to get juice) add **1 tsp honey.** Apply and remove after 15-20 minutes.

- Apply little **grape juice** on face and neck. Leave for 15-20 minutes before washing it off.

- Dip a cotton wool in some **un-boiled milk.** Pat all over face and neck. Leave for ½ hour and wash off.Lighten and Brighten Your Complexion

- Grind a few **almonds** in milk and apply on the face at bedtime.

Wash next morning or you can keep it on for ½-1 hour and wash off.

♦ Soak **chana dal (split gram) in milk** overnight. Next morning grind to a paste. Mix a
  pinch of **haldi (turmeric powder)** and a few
  drops of **lemon juice**. Apply and keep for ½
  an hour before washing it off.

♦ Mix **1 tbsp milk, 1 tsp** each of **carrot juice, orange juice** and
  honey. Apply, leave for 15-20 minutes and wash.

♦ Grate a small **potato** along with the peel. Squeeze to take out
  juice and apply the juice with a face brush on your face. Leave
  for 20 minutes till dry and then wash off.

♦ Mix **1 tbsp kheera (cucumber) juice, a few drops of lemon juice**
  and **a pinch of haldi (turmeric powder)**. Apply and keep for 25-
  30 minutes before washing.

Removing Dark Circles Around Eyes

♦ Apply **kheera (cucumber) juice or potato juice** around the eyes with a brush or cotton wool. You will find a change in 2-3 weeks. Simply grate a small potato or a 1" piece of kheera along with the peel and then squeeze within your palm to get juice. When you buy potatoes for the week, buy 7-8 small sized ones, keeping them aside and using one each day for your under eyes. Apply the juice not only under your eyes but on the complete face and neck since potatoes have a bleaching quality, keeping the face clear of blemishes.

♦ Take **1 tsp tomato juice, ½ tsp lemon juice, a pinch of haldi (turmeric powder)** and **½ tsp besan (gram flour)**. Make a paste and apply. Leave for 10 minutes and wash off.

Remove Sunburn/Suntan

♦ Mix **1 tbsp tomato juice** (grate tomato and squeeze through a muslin cloth to get juice) and **2 tbsp thick curd.** Apply with a face brush. Wash after ½ hour.

♦ Mix **1 tsp olive oil** with **1 tsp of vinegar** and apply an hour before your bath.

Shrink Open Pores

♦ Mix **1 tbsp tomato juice** and a **few drops of lemon juice.** Apply on open pores. Wash after 15-20 minutes.

♦ **Rub ice** everyday at the area where open pores are present. Wash face with cold water. Never use hot water on face.

MAGIC TIPS FOR THE MIDDLE AGED WOMEN

Dark Spots On the Cheeks

On reaching middle age, a lot of women develop dark spots on their cheeks and nose. The most effective treatment for this is to apply with a brush, a mixture of ½ **tsp multani mitti** mixed with **1 tsp radish (mooli) juice** (grate 1½" piece of radish and squeeze within your hands to get the juice).

Note: When applying the mixture, keep away from the eyes and do not apply too close to the eyes. This mixture gives a burning sensation in the eyes and on the face at the beginning, but the skin gets used to it after a few days. It may also make the skin a little reddish which soon becomes all right.

Wrinkle Free Skin

By using the tips given below, you can prevent wrinkles to make your skin younger looking and wrinkle free.

- Mix **1 tbsp carrot juice** with **1 tsp milk.** Apply on your face and neck. It removes ugly age lines from your face.

- Take **1 tbsp egg white** and **1 tsp rose water.** Add **2 drops of glycerine.** Mix well and apply on face and neck with a brush. Sit still for 20 minutes. Do not talk till mask is dry and hard. Rinse well.

- Mix **1 tsp olive oil** and **1 tbsp egg white.** Apply on face and neck and let it dry. Do not talk when this pack is on the face. Then remove it with a piece of cotton wool dipped in ½ cup hot water to which a pinch of mitha soda (soda bicarbonate) has been added.

♦ Take **½ tbsp cold malai (milk topping),** add **4-5 drops lemon juice.** Rub on your face. You can massage your face with this. Keep for 20-25 minutes and then wash off with water. **Not recommended for very oily skins.**

♦ Apply **papaya pulp** (finely grate and mash a little ripe papaya) on the face and neck. Leave for ½ hour. Along with wrinkles your blemishes will also disappear. If you find the pulp messy, eat the papaya and rub the peel which has some papaya on it, on your face and neck.

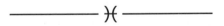

Removing Stubborn Wrinkles

Mix **1 tbsp honey** and **½ tbsp carrot juice.** To extract juice, grate a little carrot and squeeze it within your palm to get some juice. Apply on the face and neck. Leave for 20 minutes. Soak cotton wool in warm water to which a **pinch of soda bicarb (mitha soda)** has been added. Remove mask with this.

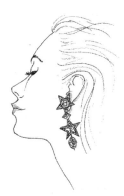

Health and Fitness

You are what you eat! A well balanced diet keeps you fit and healthy. A low-calorie, high fibre diet not only keeps extra kilos off, but also adds glow to your skin and lustre to your hair. Eat lots of vegetables, fruits and cereals in your diet. Include fresh salads in the meals.

If a proper diet is combined with some exercise, it becomes much easier to stay slim. Exercise is not boring. It is your attitude which makes it so. Select an exercise which blends with your life style, your system and your needs. Exercise firms muscles, moves joints and makes you supple. It improves circulation by increasing the intake of oxygen. And, most importantly, it relaxes the mind, delaying the ageing process.

Natural Weight Loss

NO CRASH DIETING - LOSE WEIGHT GRADUALLY

- Crash diets lower your metabolism and set the stage for gaining fat a lot faster in the future, when you come off the diet.

- Never miss a meal. If this is done, one tends to eat without thinking at the next meal, usually resulting in wrong choice of food and eating more quantity.

- Breakfast should be the biggest meal, lunch should be normal and dinner the lightest.

Slimsational Tips

Avoid Sauces and Gravies:

Traditional sauces like mayonnaise, gravies and other dressings are often made from cream, white flour and oil.

Have Faith in Mushrooms:

Button mushrooms are exceptional from every point of view, as they are an excellent fibre source and also contain many vitamins. They are low in calories too.

Drinks to be Outlawed:

Colas, fizzy drinks and ready-made fruit juices are generally made from fruit and plant extracts, which are nearly always synthetic and they always contain a lot of sugar. Avoid them.

Salt and Weight:

♦　Eating a lot of salt will make it more difficult for you to lose weight. Avoid salt in salads completely and also reduce the quantity of salt in other dishes.

♦　When you eat a lot of salt, it may cause your body to retain fluid, making it difficult for you to lose weight. Your body regulates the concentration of salt quite carefully. If you consume a lot of salt, then your body holds on to water to dilute the salt concentration to proper levels. When you first reduce the salt in your diet, the food may taste too bland, but after about two weeks, your palate gets readjusted.

The Right Choice of Diet

Eat the following foods whenever you feel hungry until you are full (but not until you are stuffed):

- **Fruits** - watermelons, pears, melons, papayas, pomegranates (anaar), apples, apricots, strawberries, cherries, oranges, peaches, guavas etc.

- **Grains** - wheat (atta, suji), corn (cornflakes), rice, oats, etc.

- **Vegetables** - potatoes, lady fingers (bhindi), broccoli, carrots, lettuce, mushrooms, eggplant, onions, fenugreek (methi), spinach, and so on.

Eat in moderation

- **Nonfat dairy products,** including skim milk, nonfat yogurt, paneer made from low fat milk, and egg whites.

- **Beans and legumes** - dals, rajmah, lobhia, channe.

Avoid as much as possible

- **Meats** (all kinds, including chicken and fish)
- **Oils** (all kinds) and oil-containing products, including margarines and most salad dressings.

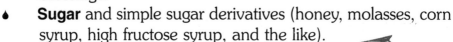

- **Sugar** and simple sugar derivatives (honey, molasses, corn syrup, high fructose syrup, and the like).
- **Alcohol**
- **Olives**
- **Nuts and seeds**
- **High-fat dairy products,** including whole milk, whole milk yogurt, butter, cheese, egg yolks, cream, khoya etc.

Tips for Low Fat Cooking

- There are cooking methods that use little or no fat — try to use them whenever you can. Choose these methods over deep frying. These include steaming, baking, broiling, grilling, and stir-frying in a small amount of oil. Even when you stir fry in small amount of fat, remember to take out the fried food on an absorbent paper napkin to remove extra oil.

- Always heat oil thoroughly before sauteing food. Why? Because cold oil is absorbed more readily than hot.

- Heat up your foods with green chillies, red chillies and hot sauces. Hot, spicy foods curb the appetite and burn slightly more calories than bland foods.

♦ If you find you can't give up the flavour of butter in certain dishes, then add just a dollop at the end of cooking. If you add it earlier in the cooking process, the flavour will be cooked away and you'll be left with just the oil.

♦ Low-cholesterol foods don't have to be tasteless and boring. Transform your low-fat cooking into exotic dishes with herbs and spices. Experiment until you find combinations you especially like. Discover ginger, nutmeg, garlic, cumin, rosemary, thyme, carom seeds (ajwain), oregano, mint, paprika, lemon juice and lemon zest, and a wide range of other herbs.

- Control the fat in cheese with smaller portions. If you grate or shred cheese, you'll use less than you would with a slice or chunk of cheese.

- Use low-calorie yogurt (dahi) in cooking. To prevent it from curdling when heated, add 1 tsp cornflour for every cup of yogurt. When adding the yogurt, reduce the heat to minimum or preferably remove the pan to which the yogurt is going to be added, from fire.

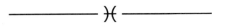

Cooking Tips

Curries:

♦ When milk or curd is to be added to tomato masala of gravies, bhuno tomatoes well till dry and oil separates before adding the curd or milk. Bhuno-ing well lessens the sourness of the tomatoes and the added milk or curd does not curdle. If the tomatoes are not well bhunoed, there are chances of getting a curdled gravy.

♦ When adding curd to curries, always remember to beat the curd. Remove the masala from fire when adding the curd or milk to the masala. Stir well to mix. Return to low heat.

- If your curry turns out a bit oily and pungent, take two bread slices and crumble them coarsely. Add this to the curry and mix well. Bread absorbs the excess oil and spice.

- If your gravy becomes too salty, make a few small balls of atta (chappati dough) and put them in the gravy. Give 2-3 boils. Let them remain for some time in the curry. Before serving remove these balls which have absorbed the extra salt.

- To thicken gravies and also add flavour to the gravy, grind 1-2 tbsp of soaked cashew nuts or almonds or magaz (watermelon seeds) or chironji to a fine paste. Add to the gravy and relish the difference it makes.

- 1 tbsp of kasoori methi (dried fenugreek leaves) added to gravies enhances the taste but a little extra may turn the gravy bitter.

Onions and Garlic:

- Place onions in the fridge for ½-1 hour before chopping them. Your eyes will not water.

- Heating the knife before cutting up onions can prevent you from shedding tears.

- Soak garlic in water for sometime. It peels easily.

- The best way to keep garlic handy is to peel all the flakes and store in a jar of oil. This flavoured oil is great for salads and seasoning.

- When using pressure cooker place the days requirement of garlic pods on its lid for 10 minutes. They will be easier to peel.

- Add salt to onion when frying (browning), they will brown fast and turn soft sooner.

- For garnishing pulaos, etc., fry onions with a pinch of sugar. They will brown faster.

Rice and Dal:

- To prevent water from overflowing while cooking rice coat the rim of the vessel with butter or ghee.

- Add 1-2 slices of lemon or a little lemon juice to rice while cooking. It keeps it white and grainy.

- Add 1 tsp of oil to rice while boiling, it will not boil over.

- Add a few drops of oil while cooking dals to reduce the cooking time and frothing.

- To 1 cup of dal, 3-4 cups of water are generally added depending on the type of dal.

Chappati and Poori:

- The dough should always be kept away covered for at least
  ½ hour after kneading. If chappatis are made immediately,
  they are not soft.

- While making chappatis, use hot water to mix the flour. The
  chappatis will turn out very soft and tasty.

- Add a little milk to the dough for fluffier puris.

- Before washing the milk utensil, knead the dough in it. You
  get a softer dough and a cleaner utensil.

- For a protein rich diet add ½ kg of soya bean flour to 3 kg wheat flour for making paranthas.

- Do not throw away the water after making paneer. Use it for making dough for chappatis, which will give softer, tastier and more nutritive chappatis.

- Spread newspaper under the rolling board (chakla) while making chappatis. All the dry flour will fall on the paper and it becomes easy to empty it into the dustbin.

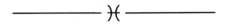

Snacks:

- Add a handful of puffed/crushed rice (chirwa or poha) to the pakora batter for extra crisp pakoras.

- Add a handful of puffed/crushed rice (chirwa or poha) to the rice while soaking for idlis. You will get fluffier idlis.

- If dosas stick to the tawa, cut an onion into half. Clean tawa with the cut side of the onion and a little oil. If this does not help, heat tawa empty very well till almost fuming. Switch off the gas. Let it cool. Then reheat and make dosas. Dosas will not stick.

- To add more flavour to dosas, add a few methi daana (fenugreek seeds) to the batter. And taste the difference!

- To make neat and crisp dosas, everytime you apply oil on the tawa, sprinkle salt water over it.

- Salt should be added to the dosa batter before it is kept for fermentation.

- Often the first dosa sticks to the tawa and refuses to come out. This can be solved by greasing the tawa with oil and a pinch of salt.

- Add a little dahi (yogurt) to dahi vada batter to get softer vadas. They will also absorb less oil while frying.

- For getting a thick, crisp coating on cutlets or rolls, dip the prepared snack in eggwhite beaten with a few tbsp of water and then roll in fine bread crumbs. If you do not take eggs, dip them in a thin batter of maida and water and then roll in bread crumbs. Fry till well browned.

- In the absence of bread crumbs, suji may be used to get a crisp coating.

- If your cutlets fall apart, dip some bread slices in water for a second, squeeze it and add to the cutlet mixture. You may also add a raw egg to the cutlet mixture for binding instead of the bread, if you take eggs.

- Wrap sandwiches without cutting the sides, in foil or cling wrap to keep them soft. Cut the crust only at the time of serving to prevent the edges from drying.

- To make crisp potato chips, soak them in cold water for 1 hour. Drain. Wipe dry and deep fry.

- To get extra crisp chips, sprinkle the soaked, dried chips with some maida (plain flour) before frying. Maida absorbs any excess water present.

- For deep frying any snack, add small quantities to the oil at one time. This maintains the oil's temperature. If too many pieces are added together, the oil turns cold and a lot of oil is then absorbed by the snack.

- After deep frying, let the oil cool down. Add a little quantity of fresh oil to used oil before reusing. This prevents oil from discolouring.

Milk:

- A pinch of salt will take away scorched taste of burnt milk. Put in the salt when the milk is still hot.

- When the summer begins and you need to prevent the milk from curdling, add half a teaspoon of soda bi-carb to 2 litres of milk, and boil.

- If you have forgotten to keep the milk in the refrigerator, you can prevent if from curdling by adding a pinch of soda bicarb to it before boiling.

- Glycerine prevents boiling over. Apply a little glycerine to the rim of the utensil in which you have put milk or anything to boil and you can literally go to sleep. This will prevent boiling or overflowing.

- While making mawa or rabri, put an inverted katori in the boiling milk. This prevents the milk from spilling over and you need not stand next to the stove to keep stirring the milk.

- A milk packet kept in the fridge for more than seven days will not get curdled on heating if heated on a very low flame.

- Custard won't burn at the bottom if sugar is added after the boiling is over and the desired consistency is attained. Of course, the sugar will dissolve easily in the hot liquid.

- For a delicious flavour in custards, add a little brandy.

- Put a little water, about 2 tbsp in the pan first before putting the milk in it to boil. This prevents the milk from getting burnt at the bottom.

Curds:

♦ If you find that the curd has not set properly, gently heat the container by immersing it in hot water. The curd that will form will be of 'rock' consistency.

♦ Curd which has not set properly, if placed in a covered dish in the sun for sometimes will set immediately and you will get thick curds.

♦ If you have a problem in setting curd during winter or in the rainy season, set curd and put the container on the voltage stabilizer of your refrigerator.

♦ If your curd has become too sour, drain off the water by tying it in a muslin cloth and hanging it for about 15 minutes. Add milk or water to the residue.

♦ If milk is too thin (rainy season) and curds don't set well, add a little milk powder to milk. Mix very well and then set curds. You will get excellent thick curds.

Cream, Cheese and Cream Cheese:

♦ To prepare cream cheese: Take one cup curds and three cups of milk. When the milk is boiling pour the curd into it and add salt to taste. Strain the mixture and place it in a bowl to cool. Do not remove all the moisture when straining, as the cheese will be too dry. When the mixture cools down, blend till smooth in a blender.

♦ Smear a little oil on the grater before grating cheese. The cheese will no longer stick to the grater.

♦ Fresh cream can be preserved for a few days in the fridge by adding a few drops of curds to it.

♦ To help whipping cream that is too thin, add a few drops of lemon juice and allow to stand for a few minutes before beating.

♦ When whipped cream is required, add the white of an egg to the cream; it will whip in half the time and the cream will be stiffer.

♦ To obtain a perfectly whipped cream for dessert toppings,

chill the beater and the cream bowl for about ½ hour before beating.

Eggs, Poultry, Meat and Fish

◆ Do not buy a chicken with yellow skin and flesh. Buy one with white skin and flesh.

◆ If you plunge the knife in cold water before slicing hard boiled eggs, the yolk will not crumble to pieces.

◆ Meat can be tenderized and flavoured by soaking in some beer for 1 hour.

◆ To tenderize meat, rub with raw papaya

paste and leave for ½-1 hour.

- While boiling tough meat, try adding a spoon of vinegar with the water. It will make it softer.

- Never refreeze thawed out meat, as it will turn hard and tough while cooking.

- To remove fish odour from a pan, sprinkle salt on the pan, add hot water and let it stand for a while before washing.

- To remove a fish bone if it sticks in your throat, gulp down lemon juice or cooked rice immediately.

- If the fish is not very fresh and smells, rub it with besan (gram flour) and keep aside for 10 minutes. Wash thoroughly with water. The fishy odour will disappear.

Vegetables:

◆ To retain the green colour of the leafy vegetables, use a few drops of lemon juice. But avoid the use of cooking soda as it robs vegetables of vitamins especially vitamin "C". Use of lemon juice, helps in conserving the goodness and brightness in vegetables.

◆ Leafy vegetables retain their natural colour if cooked in an open vessel with less water rather than in a covered one.

◆ Green vegetables will also retain their colour if you sprinkle some sugar on them while cooking.

◆ Vitamins and minerals of green vegetables lie generally close to the skin, and therefore they should be peeled thinly to

avoid waste of vitamins. Vegetables like
cucumber should be sliced with the skin
for the salad.

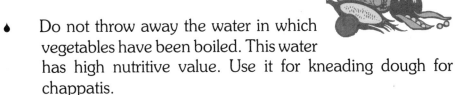

♦ Do not throw away the water in which
vegetables have been boiled. This water
has high nutritive value. Use it for kneading dough for
chappatis.

♦ Remember to take off the corn kernels off the fire as soon as
they are tender; if cooked longer they become tough again.

♦ After boiling the peas, pour cold water over them. They will
remain green and fresh.

♦ After buying vegetables for the week, keep aside one or two pieces of each vegetable, separately in a vegetable bag. Make mixed vegetables at the end of the week, when your vegetable stock has been exhausted.

- Lettuce tastes better if it is coated with a light French dressing or sprinkled with lime juice and salt.

- Never cut lettuce leaves. Tear them.

- To make lettuce crisp, stand it in water overnight in the fridge or put them in a pan of cold water with slices of a raw potato.

- Soak whole cucumbers in salt water for 1-2 hours before using. This will make them more digestible and they will absorb dressing more easily.

- If a cucumber is broken at its centre, the bitterness if any, gets eliminated.

- Don't discard the outer green coloured leaves of cabbage because they contain more vitamins and calcium.

- Wash and dry lady fingers (bhindi) thoroughly before cooking to get crisp lady fingers.

- While cooking, if the lady fingers become sticky, squeeze juice of a lemon and fry a little. They will become nice and crisp.

- To keep vegetables like ladyfingers, brinjals and boiled potatoes, crisp and crunchy after they are cooked, add salt only when the vegetable is almost done.

───────────────────────────────────────

- Brinjals when you buy should be smooth to the touch and should be of light weight. Heaviness indicates that it is overmature with plenty of seeds inside.

- Rub salt on brinjals after they are cut and place them in a colander (strainer). Rinse well after 30 minutes. This remove the slight bitterness in them and they taste much better.

- Cabbage and cauliflower should be bought on the basis of their weight. The heavier, the better. Light heads in cabbages denote poor quality.

- Green colour in bitter gourds (karela) indicates more bitterness than in the white variety.

- To remove bitterness from karelas (bitter gourds), mix 2-3 tbsp vinegar and 1 tsp salt to them and keep aside for a few hours. Squeeze well and rinse 2-3 times. Lemon juice may also be used instead of vinegar.

◆ Don't throw away mint stalks after plucking the leaves. Select thick straight stalks and plant them in your backyard or in a pot and see mint grow beautifully.

◆ Cut tomatoes vertically instead of horizontally, to keep the slices firm and retain much of their juice.

Miscellaneous:

◆ When making tikkas or tandoori vegetables, add 1 tbsp of cornflour to the marinade. It helps the marinade stick better to the paneer or the vegetable.

- When a recipe is doubled, never double the salt and other seasonings. Mostly it is 1½ times. Taste food to make sure.

- Keep dry poodina (mint) handy. Crush and add to curds and lassi, nimboo paani, salads, chopped fruits etc. It is very refreshing in summers as well as a good digestive. To make poodine waala nimboo paani, put all ingredients in the mixi along with chopped fresh or dried poodina leaves and blend to get an appetizing lemon drink.

- Do not use mitha soda (soda bicarb) while cooking channas and rajmah, because it destroys Vitamin B.

- When a bottle of chilli sauce is nearly empty, add a little olive oil, some vinegar and seasoning to taste. Mix well and use it as a salad dressing.

♦ To cut wafer-thin slices from a loaf of bread, dip the knife in boiling water or warm the blade over the fire and then cut the bread.

♦ Save grease - proof paper wrappings from your bread loaf. These sheets make ideal coverings for sandwiches, packed lunches and snacks.

♦ While giving stick ice creams to children, wrap a paper napkin around the ice cream stick. The napkin will absorb ice cream droplets and you won't have to deal with messy hands and stained clothes.

♦ If you have forgotten to soak rajmah or channas overnight, just put them in a pressure cooker with some water and give

1 whistle. Remove from fire. Cool for 15 minutes. Add more water and keep aside for 5 minutes. Then cook as usual.

How to use Gelatine in Desserts:

* Gelatine should be sprinkled over the liquid rather than adding liquid to the gelatine. When gelatine is sprinkled over the liquid & left for one or two minutes, it dissolves very easily.

* Never use gelatine which is more than a year old, so always check the manufacturing date when buying gelatine.

* Gelatine solution should never be boiled. Always heat gelatine with the liquid in a small heavy bottomed pan, on

very low heat. If the utensil in which the gelatine is to be heated is not heavy bottomed, keep it on a tawa (griddle), kept over the fire to reduce the heat further. Do not let the gelatine boil.

- Melted gelatine should never be added to cold mixtures. The gelatine begins to set in long, gluey strands. Preferably, the temperature of the gelatine solution and the mixture to which it is going to be added should be the same, conveniently both at room temperature.

- In winters, never prepare the gelatine solution in advance. It tends to set and then becomes useless. The gelatine should be dissolved and used within a few minutes during winters.

Important Tips for Baking Perfect Cakes

- Measure the ingredients with great care. Using correct amounts of ingredients is more important than the beating of the cakes.

- Invest in a good electric hand mixer. It simplifies your work besides giving good results. Always beat in one direction.

- To beat the egg whites light as air, they should be at room temperature while beating. Always use a clean, dry bowl and beater for beating.

◆ While using raisins or dry fruits or peels in a cake, first coat them with a little flour (maida) and then add to the batter. They will then not sink to the bottom of the cake.

◆ Remember to always sift the baking powder with the maida at the time of making the cake.

◆ Never use baking powder which is more than a year old. Check the manufacturing date on the container.

◆ Always preheat the oven at the temperature at which you have to bake your cake for at least 10 minutes.

◆ Always grease your baking tin and dust (sprinkle) with flour (maida).

- Baking should always be done in aluminium containers.

- Do not open the oven door again and again to check the cake as this causes variation in the temperature and hence affects the baking.

- Test your cake with a clean knife at the place where the cake has risen the most, i.e. at the highest point, before removing from the oven.

- Permit the cake to cool for sometime before you remove it from the tin.

- Never cool a cake under the fan as this will make the cake hard.

What Went Wrong With Your Cake

A Heavy Cake: Too little baking powder; too much flour; mixture not creamed enough; flour mixed too vigorously; oven too slow.

A Dry Cake: Too much baking powder or flour; not enough fat or liquid; too long in the oven.

A Sunken Cake: Too much liquid, baking powder or sugar; too little flour; oven door slammed or cake moved during baking; taken out from oven too soon.

A Peaked Cake: Insufficient fat or baking powder; too much flour; oven temperature too high.

A Badly Cracked Top: Oven too hot; cake tin too small; too much flour; not enough liquid.

Fruit Sunk to the Bottom: Fruit not properly dried; cake mixture too thin; fruit added before adding flour.

Microwave Cooking Tips

- Never over-cook food in a microwave as it becomes tough and leathery. Give the dish a little standing time before you test it, to avoid over cooking.

- Never pile food on top of each other. It cooks better, evenly and quickly when spaced apart.

- Food cooks better in a round container than in a square one. In square or rectangular bowls, food gets overcooked at the corners.

- Do not add salt at the time of starting the cooking as it leads to increase in the cooking time.

- Do not add more water than required, however a little water must be added to prevent dehydration of the vegetable, which results in the loss of natural juices. Addition of extra water increase the cooking time.

- ♦ Do not deep fry in a microwave (the temperature of oil cannot be controlled).

- ♦ Do not cook eggs in their shells (pressure will cause them to explode).

- ♦ Do not cook and reheat puddings having alcohol (they can easily catch fire).

- ♦ Do not use containers with restricted openings, such as bottles.

- ♦ Use deep dishes to prepare gravies, filling the dish only 3/4 to avoid spillage.

- ♦ Do not defrost canned foodstuff.

- ♦ Do not use aluminium foil for covering dishes. Do not reheat foods (sweets like ladoos, burfi etc.) with silver sheet, as it leads to sparking.

- ♦ Fill the cake tin 3/4 with cake batter, allowing space for cake to rise.

Useful Kitchen Tips

- Tea and coffee stains on cups will disappear if rubbed with damp salt or damp soda- bicarb (mitha soda).

- For sparkling glassware, rinse in water to which some vinegar has been added.

- Clean milk bottles and thermos flasks with water in which a little soda bicarb has been added.

- After prolonged use, non stick pans acquire a thin layer of stains and blotches. To remove these, boil 3 cups water with 1 tbsp of vinegar, 1 tbsp bleaching powder and 1 tbsp salt in the stained pan for 5-8 minutes. Scrub gently with a scrubber and wash with soap water as usual to get a clean pan.

- To wash a greasy pans or kadhais, rub with some gramflour (besan) first. Then wash with soap. The grease will come off easily.

- To sharpen the blades of your mixi put some table salt in it. Run it for a while.

- Line your freezer shelf with wax paper to prevent ice trays from sticking to it.

- To remove egg smell from crockery, rub with used tea leaves or rinse with a little vinegar.

- Clean stained melmoware crockery by soaking it for ½ hour in a tubful of hot water to which 2 cups of liquid bleach has been added.

- Separate stuck tumblers by putting ice cold water in the inner one. It will contract in size (minutely, of course) and easily slip out.

- To keep your fridge smelling fresh ensure that food spills are cleaned immediately and not allowed to accumulate in the crevices, corners or gaskets. If you plan to go away and switch off the fridge, first empty the fridge and clean thoroughly. Leave the fridge door partially open to allow circulation of air.

- If your kitchen sink gets blocked, add some pieces of un-ground salt and leave it overnight.

- Keep empty storage tins or bottles upside down on the shelf so that you can spot them immediately when you need them.

- To get rid of kerosene odour, wash hands with curds.

- If you burn fingers while holding a hot vessel, just put them on the ice in your freezer. There will be no blisters or marks.

Party Tips

Substitutes: Sometimes it happens that one suddenly realizes that one ingredient is missing. The following are handy substitutes.

Item	Substitutes
1 tbsp cornflour	2 tbsp maida (as thickening agent)
1 tsp baking powder	2 tsp soda bicarb (mitha soda)
1 cup fresh milk	4 tbsp powdered whole milk + 1 cup water
1 cup cream	3/4 cup skimmed milk and 1/3 cup butter
30 gm chocolate (solid)	3 tbsp cocoa + 1 tsp fat
2 tsp arrowroot	2 tbsp flour (as a thickening, also gives a gloss)
1 cup self raising flour	1 cup flour + 2 tsp baking powder
2 tsp drinking chocolate	1 tsp cocoa + 1 tsp sugar

Approximate Quantities Required For A Party

Item	Serving	Quantity
Tea	25 cups	40 gms tea leaves
Coffee	25 cups	75 gms instant coffee
Squash	20 glasses	1 bottle
Bread	24 slices	1 large
Sandwiches	24 pieces	1 large bread
Butter	24 slices	100 gms
Rice (Basmati)	4 servings	1 cup
Rice (Basmati)	25 people	1 kg
Dry vegetable preparation	25 people	2 kg
Dals	25 people	2 cups
Potato Chips	25 people	1 kg
Ice cream	25 people	3 litres
Cake	25 people	1½ kg

Weights and Measures

Use a tea cup for measuring

A table spoon is written as tbsp, a teaspoon as tsp.

Food stuff	Measure	Weight (gms)
Cereals		
Rice	1 cup	125
Atta (wheat flour)	1 cup	100
Maida (plain flour)	1 cup	100
Suji	1 cup	120
Dals (Pulses)		
Average for all dals	$^1/_3$ cup	50
Rajmah	1 cup	125
Channa	1 cup	125
Besan	$^3/_4$ cup	50

Food stuff	Measure	Weight (gms)
Dairy Products		
Milk	1 cup	200
Milk Powder	¼ cup	20
Cheese grated	1 tbsp	5
Butter	1 cup	150
	1 tbsp	15
Curd	½ cup	100
	1 tbsp	15
Cream	½ cup	100
	1 tbsp	15
Fats and Oils		
Refined oil	1 cup	150
	1 tbsp	15
Ghee	1 cup	180
	1 tbsp	15

Food Storing and Freezing

◆ Store tomatoes whole in the freezer. They remain fresh for months. To use, remove and when slightly thawed, peel. Mash or chop and use. (These cannot be used for salad or for eating raw.)

◆ To keep mushrooms fresh, remove from plastic packet, wrap in brown paper and keep in the fridge. They will stay fresh for 2-3 days. Never keep mushrooms in the freezer.

◆ Grind fresh green chillies with a little vinegar and pinch of salt (optional). Store in small boxes. Keep in the freezer. Remove one box at a time for use and keep in the freezer.

- Ginger and garlic pastes can be made and stored like chillies except that make the paste (grind) with little water to get a smooth paste.

- Add a piece of gur (jaggery) to the ghee container to keep it fresh for a longer time.

- Store eggs with the broad ends up. Yolks are less likely to break after storage this way.

- Keep mint leaves, lettuce leaves, parsley and coriander leaves in water in the fridge. Will remain fresh and crisp for 2-3 days. Ideal for salads and garnishing.

- Put a little cooking oil on the chappati dough and then store, covered in the fridge. This prevents a crust from forming on the top.

Cooking Ideas

- If storing masalas for a couple of months (masala like red chilli powder, dhania powder, etc.) always store in glass bottles. Add a few pieces of garlic cloves to prevent fungus and insects.

- Place small pieces of hing (asafoetida) in containers of haldi (turmeric) powder or dhania (coriander) powder to protect from worms.

- To keep worms and insects away from stored rice, mix some dried red chillies or garlic flakes in it.

- To keep ants away from sugar, add a few laung (cloves) in the sugar tin.

- To keep away dampness from flour (atta) tuck a bay leaf into the container. The dried leaf will absorb moisture.

- To prevent dals from insects, clean and rub a little oil on the dals before storing them.

- Roast suji (semolina) for 5 minutes before storing it to keep it free of worms.

- If you are planning a long holiday away from home, empty the fridge and keep the door slightly open to avoid the formation of fungus inside.

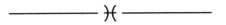

Home-Keeping

It's always a pleasure to visit a house which is well maintained. Keep your silver and brass articles shinning and bright and crockery sparkling clean. Look after your indoor plants and flowers so that they always remain fresh. Keep your window panes clean and carpets new forever. Make your kitchen free of cockroaches. Turn your home into your dream house.

Proper care of clothes makes clothes look new even after several washes. Well looked after clothes enhance your personality giving you a neat, chic appearance. There is no need to keep running to the dry cleaners all the time. Learn the art of looking after your expensive pashminas, favourite silks and other clothes.

Care of Clothes

Washing Clothes

For clothes whose colour runs:

Soak in detergent with **1-2 tsp Borax powder.** The colours will not coat one another (If it is lemon and blue, the blue will not go on to the lemon and vice versa).

Soak in detergent with **2-3 tbsp vinegar and 2-3 tsp salt.**

Woolens and Silks:

Woolens and silks should be **washed in cold water** and with gentle detergents. Do not wring to dry. Instead, **roll in a towel** to soak up moisture. Then **dry in the shade.** Silks can be hung but woolens can lose shape on hanging. Dry woolens on a flat surface. This way there will be no distortion in the shape of these garments.

To **soften woolens** add a little **glycerine** to the last rinse.

After washing silk clothes, add a little **lime juice** to the final rinse. They will retain their **shine.**

Denims and Corduroy:

Wash denims and corduroy **turned inside out.** This will prevent colour streaking in jeans and keep the nap (woolly surface) up in corduroys.

Soft Towels:

To soften towels and other cottons add a few tablespoons of **vinegar.** The acidity will counteract the alkalinity imparted in the washing and bring back the natural softness.

Dark Fabrics:

Dry dark fabrics inside out to prevent colour from fading due to sunlight.

Dirty Shirt Cuffs and Collars:

To remove grime from shirt cuffs and collars, rub **talcum powder** on them liberally till it forms a thick coating and leave it overnight. Wash as usual the next day and watch the dirt come off easily.

Removing Stains from Clothes

Blood Stains: Soak in **cold water** to which some **salt** is added for at least 1 - 1½ hrs. Rinse wash with soap and cold water. **Never soak blood stain in hot water as it will harden the stain.**

Fruit Stains (stains of mango and pomegranate): Take **glycerine** in a flat shallow dish and dip the stained part only, for 24 hours. Then scrub and wash with a soft brush, soap and water.

Tea, Coffee and Cocoa: Fresh stains can be removed if sponged immediately with cold water. Old stains can be removed by steeping (soaking) the garment in a hot solution of **1 tbsp borax powder mixed with 1 cup hot water (250 ml)** for about 10 minutes or till cool. Rinse and wash.

Pan Stains: Rub eating **chuna paste** on the stains and rub. Wash as usual.

Haldi Stains: Rub the spot/stain of haldi with soap and a little water. Do not wash. Keep in the sunlight till dry. Then wash, the stain will come out.

Chewing Gum: To remove chewing gum from clothes, rub with **ice.**

Ink Stains: Soak the stain in **milk** for sometime. Another way to remove ink stains is to rub **sour curd** on the stain. Wait till stain disappears and then wash away. Yet another way to remove ink stains from clothes is to soak them in a solution of **lime juice and salt** for a few minutes before washing.

Grease or Oil Stain:

Put **talcum powder** on the stain as soon as possible. Leave for sometime. Then **iron** the stain by keeping **blotting paper above and below** the stain.

Lipstick on your Collar? Don't worry. Lipstick stains can be removed by rubbing a little **glycerine** and leaving it on for a while.

Ice-cream stains: Wash the clothes with water, apply a little **borax powder.** Keep for 5 minute and wash off.

Perspiration Stains: Perspiration stains on clothes will disappear if you add a couple of **aspirins** to the water while washing them.

Storing & Preserving Expensive Clothes

For Storing Pashmina/Shatoosh shawls: Make small bundles of (cloves) laung in a muslin cloth and keep in between the folds of the shawls.

Mildew-Fungus (ulli, phaphundi): To Prevent mildew developing on stored clothes **don't use starch** on the items as it attracts mildew. Moisture too encourages mildew. Dampness in closets can be reduced by **hanging a bundle of 12 or more writing chalks,** tied with a string, inside the closet. The chalks will absorb some of the moisture.

To Prevent Moth Damage: Clean clothes, specially woolens, thoroughly to **remove moth eggs** that may be present, before you put them away. Cleaning also removes perspiration, food particles and dirt, all of which attract insects.

Scatter moth balls on top of the garments stored away in the **trunk,** as the vapours being heavier than air, will only settle down.

For clothes stored in a **closet** you can put **moth balls in old socks** and suspend them over the garments as bags.

Care of Carpets

- For carpets silk/woolen, keep **dried neem leaves** in them. Instead of neem, **tobacco** (cheap variety) can also be used.

- If you have wall to wall carpeting, sprinkle **tobacco leaves** available in the market below the carpet. Repeat every 2 years. The carpet will be well protected.

- Place a layer of **newspapers** under your carpet. This will prevent if from getting damp, especially during the monsoon.

Cleaning and Upkeep of Things Around The House

● For shining silverware, soak them in water to which 2-3 tsp baking soda/soda bicarb and 2-3 tsp salt has been added. Wipe dry and polish with ordinary tooth paste (not the gels.)

● Copper and brass articles can be cleaned with salt and vinegar. Moisten a wad with vinegar, dab some salt on the wad and rub vigorously. A piece of lemon also, dipped in some cleaning powder & scrubbed on the brass or copper article makes it shine.

● Glass panes are easily cleaned using a sheet of dampened newspaper (folded four times). Keep refolding the page as it collects dirt. Newspaper is an absorbent material and so picks up dirt particles.

- Electrical switches are safely cleaned with some spirit on a wad of cotton wool. It makes them look new.

- Once a fortnight, after the usual dusting of wooden furniture and articles, scrub them with a cloth sprinkled with kerosene. The furniture will shine as if new, and will also be protected from insets.

- Plastic surfaces as in transistor radios, cassette recorder, etc. can also be cleaned with some whisky or rum; brandy or vodka will do fine too!

- Beating door-mats raises quite a dust storm which may not be desirable. Try stamping on them with your feet. All the dust will fall and collect right under it. And if you place a sheet of newspaper under the mat you have a disposable dust collector.

- Ball pen ink on your hands? Put a few drops of vegetable oil over then stain and rub away with cotton wool or a bit of cloth. It works.

◆ Chewing gum on the carpet? Don't pull it out till you harden it by chilling it with an ice cube. It then becomes possible to remove it wholly. Use the same method for chocolate and candle wax drips.

◆ To dust furniture and small knick knacks, pull an old cotton sock over your hand and dust away.

◆ Once a week, water your green plants with the soap water in which your clothes are soaked. This will make your plants look greener.

◆ Add half a tablet of disprin to the water in your flower vase. The flowers will remain fresh and last for a longer time.

Get Rid of Household Pests

- While wiping the dining table with a cloth after meals, put a little salt on the damp cloth. This prevents flies from sitting on the table.

- To get rid of flies, take a slice of bread and spread a little jam over it. Sprinkle some baygon granules on it. The flies will throng to the plate and die instantly.

- A blue night bulb will keep the mosquitoes out of your room.

- To get rid of flies and mosquitoes, keep some poodina (mint) or tulsi (Holy basil) leaves on the kitchen table.

- If you find white ants crawling in holes and cracks, add 1 tsp of hing (asafoetida) to 1 cup of water and pour on them. Repeat for 2-3 days. Within a few days they will disappear.

♦ Sick and tired of those awful cockroaches in your kitchen? Take all the vessels out of the room, and wash and clean your kitchen thoroughly. Then spray a little Gamaxene powder which is freely available in the market. You will see the cockroaches literally fleeing the place.

♦ To ward off lizards, place egg shells on your kitchen window or any place of your choice.

♦ To kill the ticks that are bothering your pet, make a paste of neem leaves and apply all over the pet's body. Bathe it after a few hours. This will do the trick.

Guarding Against Burglars

- Professional burglars only enter a house if they believe it is not occupied. They look for signs of milk bottles, stuffed mailboxes, delivered newspaper, a lonesome car, dark houses with lighted entrance, or with a single living room light, open garage door etc.

- When leaving for an evening, leave some lights burning, perhaps a radio playing. When leaving for an extended period, have mail and other deliveries, newspaper etc. held or suspended and don't draw shades. Have your phone disconnected so that on-the-spot telephone check to find out if you are at home, can't be made. Don't publicize your vacation to neighbours and friends.

♦ If you are the only adult male member of the house and are going out and not returning the same night or for a couple of nights or more, make sure to tell your people at home in a domestic conversational way, in the presence of your neighbours and others that you are returning the same evening.

Fighting Fire

- When a fire breaks out don't panic. Follow these safety rules:

- Remember all fires start as small fires. If you see one, try to put it out yourself, and at the same time shout "fire......fire.....fire" to attract other's attention.

- Don't rush away from the scene of fire to bring help.

- If you have to vacate the building do it in an orderly manner. This is important. If suddenly too many people decide to rush through the same door, the exit will get jammed.

- When the electricity supply gets tripped or is switched off for any reason, don't use the lift to go down. Moreover, the lift shaft being common to all floors, gets filled with smoke.

Always go down by the stair case. It is good to count the floors one has gone down, to know when you have reached the ground floor.

♦ To keep the emergency staircase shaft smoke-free, it is important that the doors on each floor are always kept shut, but never locked.

♦ If you are trapped inside, don't panic. Most fire casualties are not because of fire, but because of suffocation from the smoke. Smoke being hot, does not exist near the flooring. So put a cloth preferably wet, to your face and crawl out of the area.

♦ If you paste the above six points on the inside of toilet doors, there's good chance that it will be read at leisure and remembered when needed!

Do's and Don'ts for Parents

The following do's and don'ts will help you in improving your relationship with your children.

◆ Show affection. A soothing touch, a loving hug, an encouraging pat and some loving words can make a world of a difference to your relationship with your children.

◆ Give them a lot of attention and importance. Sit with them and patiently listen to their problems. Treat them as friends and respect them.

◆ Never scold or criticize them in front of friends or relatives as this will result in negative feelings in the child towards the parents.

- Always trust them. Make them feel like adults by giving them responsibilities and ask their suggestions in solving family problems.

- Don't ever tell lies to them as this will set a bad example for them to follow.

- Never quarrel or abuse in front of children, for it gives them a sense of inferiority complex and insecurity.

- Don't compare them with your friend's children, or their own siblings, for they will feel jealous and dislike you.

- Don't be the detective in knowing their inner secrets, that are never meant to be told to you.

- Never be overprotective. Make them feel independent and trust them to do things on their own.

BEST SELLERS IN QUICK & EASY SERIES

DADI MAA KE NUSKHE

DADI MAA KE KUCH AUR NUSKHE

DADI MAA KE फलों KE NUSKHE

LOOK BEAUTIFUL

LOSE WEIGHT

Children's Birthday Parties

REIKI

Roses, Chrysanthemums, Dahlias

BEAUTY SECRETS

BEST SELLERS IN QUICK & EASY SERIES

Feng Shui

FENG SHUI SYMBOLS

Feng SHUI for your OFFICE & FACTORY

MANNERS & ETIQUETTE

STAY SLIM...EAT RIGHT

BE A WINNER!

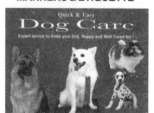

DOG CARE

VAASTU

YOGA